B.I.B.L.E
Be Involved Bible Learners Everyone

A Children's Bible Study

Cathy A. Liening

CSS Publishing Company, Inc., Lima, Ohio

B.I.B.L.E.
BE INVOLVED BIBLE LEARNERS EVERYONE

Copyright © 2008 by
CSS Publishing Company, Inc.
Lima, Ohio

The original purchaser may photocopy material in this publication for use as it was intended (worship material for worship use; educational material for classroom use; dramatic material for staging or production). No additional permission is required from the publisher for such copying by the original purchaser only. Inquiries should be addressed to: Permissions, CSS Publishing Company, Inc., 517 South Main Street, Lima, Ohio 45804.

Most scripture quotations are from the New Revised Standard Version of the Bible, copyright 1989 by the Division of Christian Education of the National Council of the Churches of Christ in the USA. Used by permission.

Scripture quotations marked (RSV) are from the Revised Standard Version of the Bible, copyrighted 1946, 1952 ©, 1971, 1973, by the Division of Christian Education of the National Council of the Churches of Christ in the USA. Used by permission.

For more information about CSS Publishing Company resources, visit our website at www.csspub.com or email us at csr@csspub.com or call (800) 241-4056.

Cover design by Barbara Spencer
ISBN-13: 978-0-7880-2504-4
ISBN-10: 0-7880-2504-X

PRINTED IN USA

To my four children
who originally inspired me to create this program
and to my husband and grandchildren
who reaffirm my favorite Bible verse:

All things do work to the good of those
who love the Lord.
— Romans 8:28

Table Of Contents

Introduction — 7

Materials Inclusion List — 9

Children's Sermons
    1 Corinthians 16:14 — 11
    Philippians 4:4 — 13
    John 3:16 — 15
    1 John 4:19 — 17
    2 Corinthians 9:15 — 19
    Hebrews 13:8 — 20
    John 11:35 — 22
    James 1:22 — 24
    Philippians 4:13 — 26
    1 Thessalonians 5:17 — 28
    1 Thessalonians 5:25 — 30
    Luke 12:34 — 32
    Psalm 119:105 — 34
    Our Favorites — 36

B.I.B.L.E. Chairperson Checklist — 37

Sample Letter To Christian Educators — 39

Sample Bulletin/Newsletter Announcements — 41

B.I.B.L.E. Display Ideas — 45

B.I.B.L.E. Procedure Explanation Poster — 47

B.I.B.L.E. Volunteer Sign-Up Sheet — 49

Bible Verses For Little Ones Master Sheet — 51

More Suggested Verses For B.I.B.L.E. Master Sheet — 53

Master List And Name Tag Example Sheet   55

Memory Paper Example Sheet   57

Memory Paper Master Sheet   59

Name Tag Master Sheet   61

Sample Certificate   63

Introduction

The art of memorization is all but gone in this age of calculators and computers. There are times when having something committed to memory helps us in life. The children's sermon series titled **B.I.B.L.E.** or **Be I**nvolved **B**ible **L**earners **E**veryone includes fourteen children's sermons and a companion program designed to encourage the congregation to learn more about God's word by memorizing a verse each week. The children's sermons revolve around a specific verse in which the presenter creates a mini-Bible study using props, songs, or activities. We used this over the summer months, but the material is relevant to any season.

The companion program challenges the participants on an intergenerational level to memorize at least one verse per week, watching their name move through the twelve-week display. Ideas for conducting the program, display helps, master pages for copying, bulletin/newsletter announcements, a sample letter, the children's sermons, and much more are shown throughout this book. This children's sermon series and program can be utilized by clergy, Christian educators, Sunday school staff, and youth workers.

The sight of small children reciting verses to grandparents, and teens reading the Bible creates a contagious effect on others excited to join the challenge. Spotlight the talents of your congregation to make this program your own. For example, invite an artistic member to create twelve posters depicting the life of Christ to use in your display, or have the youth in your church make name tags shaped like Bibles with ribbon bookmarks down the center. Read through the book carefully to utilize other suggestions on how to tailor this program to your needs. Have a special time filled with learning more about God's word while enjoying and sharing the process with family and friends.

Materials Inclusion List

This program is designed to encourage the congregation to learn more about God's word by memorizing a different Bible verse each week during a twelve-week study.
Included materials:

- Fourteen Children's Sermons
- B.I.B.L.E. Chairperson Checklist
- Sample Letter To Christian Educators
- Sample Bulletin/Newsletter Announcements
- B.I.B.L.E. Display Ideas
- B.I.B.L.E. Procedure Explanation Poster
- B.I.B.L.E. Volunteer Sign-Up Sheet
- Bible Verses For Little Ones Master Sheet
- More Suggested Verses For B.I.B.L.E. Master Sheet
- Master List And Name Tag Example Sheet
- Memory Paper Example Sheet
- Memory Paper Master Sheet
- Name Tag Master Sheet
- Sample Certificate

Learning more about the Bible can be a meaningful experience for everyone, lighting the path of life with God's love, wisdom, and guidance.

Date: _____
Introduction Week

1 Corinthians 16:14

Let all that you do be done in love.
— **1 Corinthians 16:14**

Note: The name tags, memory papers, memory box, Bible Verses For Little Ones sheets, and More Suggested Verses for B.I.B.L.E. sheets are at the back of the church under the twelve posters on which the name tags will be displayed as they are completed.

Materials: a Bible, a sample name tag, a guitar (optional)

Call the children forward, ask them to sit down and sing the song "The B-I-B-L-E."

```
      G                   C
The B-I-B-L-E, yes, that's the book for me.
      D                          G
I stand alone on the word of God, the B-I-B-L-E.
```

What does the word memorize mean? *(let them answer)* Webster's Dictionary defines memorize as "to learn by heart." Has anyone ever memorized anything? *(let them answer)* You may have learned your address, phone number, or how to spell your name. It is also important to memorize God's word. Has anyone ever memorized a Bible verse? *(let them answer)*

That's what B.I.B.L.E. is all about. We are challenged to memorize one Bible verse a week. Our program is called **Be Involved Bible Learners Everyone** or **B.I.B.L.E.** Do you see the posters in the back of church? There are twelve of them, one for each week. Every time you memorize a verse, your name tag, like this one *(show the sample name tag)*, will move up to the next poster. You can memorize as many as you like. You don't have to stop at twelve. Everyone is invited to join the fun: parents, grandparents, teenagers, college students, neighbors, and friends. There will be someone at the display before and after church each week to listen to your verse and write it down on your name tag. Your parents or another adult can listen, too, and fill out one of these memory papers and put it in the memory box. Someone will record it and make sure your name moves up for each verse you memorize.

I'll read our verse for today from the Bible. It's in the New Testament, the book called 1 Corinthians, chapter 16, verse 14. *Let all that you do be done in love. (have them repeat)* What do you think that means? *(let them answer)* We want to remember to be loving and kind in all of our actions. Let's say it together. *Let all that you do be done in love.*

It's important to remember where a verse comes from in the Bible. Let's say that together. *1 Corinthians 16:14.* That way we know where to find it in the Bible. Practice this verse at home, say it every day and live it. Next week, go to the display, recite the verse, and have your name tag placed under the first poster.

At the display are papers with Bible Verses For Little Ones and More Suggested Verses For B.I.B.L.E. Please take these home if you would like some help in picking out verses to memorize.

Let's all sing "The B-I-B-L-E" one more time.

Prayer

Thank you God for your word. Thank you for this time to learn more about you. Amen.

Date:
Week 1

Philippians 4:4

Rejoice in the Lord always; again I will say, Rejoice. — Philippians 4:4

Materials: a stack of different versions of Bibles

Has anyone ever gone to a Bible study? *(let them answer)* What do you think a Bible study is? *(let them answer)* A Bible study can mean many things, but mostly it's a time where you try to understand what God says to us about life and how to live through reading the Bible. You can study the Bible in a group, during church listening to the sermon and the lessons, at someone's house, or by yourself. We're having a Bible study right now.

Do you see all of these books? They all look really different, don't they? Do you know that they are all the same book? They are all the Bible, just different versions. Some are in modern language, some were written for children with pictures, some are in English, and some are in different languages.

There are thousands of different types of Bibles, but they all have the same message. I'll read the verse we are going to talk about today from the Bible. It's in the New Testament, in the book called Philippians, chapter 4, verse 4. *Rejoice in the Lord always; again I will say, Rejoice.* *(have them repeat)* What do you think this verse means? *(let them answer)*

There are lots of things we can rejoice in or be happy about, isn't there? Let's name some. *(let them respond)* One very special thing we can be happy about is that we can read the Bible and learn about God. Let's say our verse together. *Rejoice in the Lord always; again I will say, Rejoice — Philippians 4:4.* (Optional: Sing the song "Rejoice In The Lord, Always.")

Prayer

Dear God, help us to remember to rejoice with you and be thankful. Amen.

Date:
Week 2

John 3:16

For God so loved the world that he gave his only Son, so that everyone who believes in him may not perish but may have eternal life.

— John 3:16

Materials: a Bible, a bag of assorted nuts, a peanut shell with paper inside with the words "John 3:16: The Bible in a nutshell" written on it

Remember last week when we had all the different Bibles? Each was a little different, but all of them are a great source of God's word. I brought a bag of assorted nuts with me today. *(show them the bag with the nuts inside)* There are peanuts, cashews, pistachios, and walnuts. They all taste and look a little different, but they are all nuts and a great source of protein, except this one. What's in this one? *(open peanut shell and show them the paper)* It's certainly not a nut. It's a piece of paper. Let's see what it says. "John 3:16: The Bible in a nutshell."

Let's read this verse and see what it is. I'll read it from the Bible. It's in the New Testament, the book of John, chapter 3, verse 16. Do you see how thick the Bible is? It's a very big book, isn't it? Well, this one verse is sometimes called the Bible in a nutshell because the main message of the Bible is in this one verse. Tell me what you think this verse means. *(Read the whole verse, have them repeat, then go back and read a section at a time and have the children share their thoughts.)* God loves us so much that he sent his Son, Jesus, to be like us, to teach us how to live, and even to die for us so we might have eternal life with God. That is a wonderful message and a great verse to memorize. This is our verse for this week. Let's say it together. *For God so loved the world that he gave his only son, so that everyone who believes in him may not perish but may have eternal life — John 3:16.*

Prayer

God, thank you for your word, thank you for Jesus and your message of love, and thank you for always being with us. Amen.

Date: _____
Week 3

1 John 4:19

We love, because he first loved us.
— 1 John 4:19

Materials: a Bible, knitting needles, yarn, and a sweater

Did you know I could knit? Strangest thing, one day I saw these needles and some yarn *(show them the knitting needles and yarn)* and I picked them up and after a little while I had knitted this sweater! *(show them the sweater)* Do you believe that's what really happened? *(let them answer)* No. The truth is that I would need someone to teach me how to knit. It could not just happen; it would take many weeks for me to learn, and many more months until I could finish the sweater. I would be able to knit only if someone would first teach me.

How many of you can do something because someone else taught you? *(let them answer)* Learning isn't always easy, is it? It can takes hours and hours of practice to become really good at something. It's great to have someone teaching us who encourages and helps us while we learn. Our verse for today tells us something we do because God first taught us. I'll read it from the Bible. It's in the New Testament, the book called 1 John, chapter 4, verse 19. *We love, because he first loved us.* *(have them repeat)* How does God teach us to love? *(let them answer)* What are some ways we can love others? *(let them answer)*

Let's say that verse together. *We love because he first loved us — 1 John 4:19.*

God is the best teacher in the whole universe. God gives us love with every breath we take and shows us how to love through the Bible, through Jesus, and through all the things we experience in life.

Prayer
God, thank you for loving us and not giving up on us. Thank you for being there to help us learn to love more each day. Amen.

Date: _____
Week 4

2 Corinthians 9:15

Thanks be to God for his indescribable gift!
— 2 Corinthians 9:15

Materials: a Bible, gift-wrapped boxes

What if I told you I had some really fabulous presents in these boxes *(show them the boxes)*, like tickets to an amusement park, an iPod, or a ten-speed bike? Would you be excited to get one of these gifts? How would you thank me? *(let them answer)*
If you got one of these gifts, it would be really important to say thank you in some way wouldn't it? Well, these beautifully wrapped boxes are empty. I don't have any gifts in them, because I want to talk with you about gifts that are even better than anything that might come in a box — special gifts that God gives us. What do you think I mean? *(let them answer)* Did you know these are all gifts from God?
I'll read our verse for today from the Bible. It's in the New Testament, the book of 2 Corinthians, chapter 9, verse 15. **Thanks be to God for his indescribable gift!** *(have them repeat)* How can we thank God for all the wonderful gifts we receive every day? *(let them answer)* It's really important to remember to thank God for the gifts we have. This is the verse for this week. Let's say it together. **Thanks be to God for his indescribable gift! — 2 Corinthians 9:15.**

Prayer
God, we can never thank you enough for all that we have from you. Help us to remember to be thankful and to share your good gifts with others. Amen.

Date: _____
Week 5

Hebrews 13:8

Jesus Christ is the same yesterday and today and forever.
— Hebrews 13:8

Materials: a Bible, samples of gifts that have broken or worn out with time (tennis shoe with hole and broken laces, sweater with hole in elbow, socks with hole in heel, empty box of candy, or similar items)

These were my favorite pair of shoes. *(show them the shoes)* They don't look very good anymore, do they? I wore these almost every day, but shoes don't last forever. Oh, and here's my favorite sweater. *(show them the sweater)* I've worn it so much there's a hole in the elbow. Too bad, because I really like this sweater. Here's a box of candy. *(show them the empty candy box)* I'd share some with you, but it's all gone. Have any of you ever gotten a gift that either broke or wore out? *(let them answer)*
God gave us a wonderful gift that will never break or wear out. God gave us a special gift that is the same yesterday, today, and forever. Do you know what that gift is? Jesus! I'll read our verse for today from the Bible. It's from the New Testament, the book of Hebrews, chapter 13, verse 8. ***Jesus is the same yesterday and today and forever.*** *(have them repeat)* What do you think that verse means? *(let them answer)* Jesus and his love and caring for us never changes, does it? Jesus loves us always and that will never change. Let's say this verse together. ***Jesus is the same yesterday and today and forever — Hebrews 13:8.***

Prayer
　Thank you, God, for sending Jesus. Thank you for always loving us and caring for us. May our love for you continue from yesterday to today and forever. Amen.

Date: _____
Week 6

John 11:35

Jesus wept. — John 11:35 (RSV)

Materials: a Bible, a stack of tissue boxes

Does anyone know what's in all of these boxes? *(show them the tissue boxes and let them answer)* Tissues! That's right. This one has blue tissues, this one has 120 tissues, this one is small, and this one is large. What do we do with tissues? *(let them answer)*

Our Bible verse for today is kind of about tissues. It's also known as one of the shortest verses in the Bible. I'll read it from the Bible. It's in the New Testament, the book of John, chapter 11, verse 35. *Jesus wept. (have them repeat)* Will you say that with me? *(let them repeat the verse with you)* What does the word "wept" mean? *(let them answer)* That's right, it means "to cry." This verse is telling us that Jesus was crying. Do you know why Jesus was crying? *(let them answer)* Well, if we read the verses before this one we find out that a very dear friend of Jesus had died. The friend's name was Lazarus. He had two sisters named Mary and Martha, and when they came up to Jesus and Jesus saw them crying, he began to cry with them. Does anyone know what happened next? Jesus called to Lazarus and raised him from the dead. Lazarus was alive again. I'm sure that there were tears of joy when they saw Lazarus walking toward them.

A very good friend of mine died a while ago and I was very sad. This verse and story in the Bible helped me because I knew that Jesus understood how I felt. I've also had tears of joy in my life, like when my child was born, I went to a wedding, or I saw a beautiful sunset. I'm very thankful to Jesus for the times of joy that I've had. We'll probably all go through a few boxes of tissues in our lives because life brings us both sad and happy times. We have a Lord and Savior who knows how it feels, who understands our hurts, who says, "It's okay to cry, I'm right there by your side." Jesus can also turn our tears of sorrow into tears of joy. Jesus does understand and will always love us and be with us.

Let's say the verse again. *Jesus wept — John 11:35* (**RSV**).

Prayer

Dear Jesus, thank you for living on this earth for us and understanding us. Thank you for drying our tears, surrounding us with your love, and turning moments of sadness into joy. Amen.

Date: _____
Week 7

James 1:22

But be doers of the word, and not merely hearers who deceive themselves. — James 1:22

Materials: a Bible, a plugged-in iron, earplugs, earmuffs, a sealed envelope with a card that says, "Don't forget to unplug the iron in the front of church so it does not catch on fire."

    I have received a special message that I'd like someone to read to me because it's very important that I do what it says. *(Pick a child to read or have an adult if children are too young.)* You need to make sure I follow what the message says. But first, let me put these earplugs in and my earmuffs on. *(put them on)* Now go ahead and read the message. Something is wrong; I couldn't hear a thing you said. *(let them tell you what the problem is)* What? Oh, take off the earmuffs and the earplugs. Okay, try it again. *(Have the child or adult read the message again. Do not unplug the iron, just start talking about something else.)* I like the color on these earmuffs. That reminds me, did anyone hear what the weather is going to be like today? *(Say a few more sentences until someone says something about the iron.)* Yes, I heard the message. Unplug the iron, so what? I took off the earmuffs and earplugs. I heard the message. Oh, I need to do what the message says. Why is that so important? *(let them answer)* That's right, so the church doesn't burn down and everyone will be safe. It is important that I not only hear the message, but that I do what it says. I need to hear it and do it. *(Unplug the iron and put it in safe place.)*
    Our verse for today is about the same exact thing. I'll read it from the Bible. It's in the New Testament, the book of James, chapter 1, verse 22. *But be doers of the word, and not merely hearers who*

deceive themselves. *(have them repeat)* Be doers of the word. What word? *(let them answer)* That's right, it means the Bible. What does this verse mean? *(let them answer)* We need to read God's word and listen to God's word, but we need to take action and follow what God tells us to do. What are some things God tells us to do in the Bible? *(let them answer)* This one verse is telling us a lot. Let's say it together again. ***But be doers of the word, and not merely hearers who deceive themselves — James 1:22.***

The last part of the verse, not merely hearers who deceive themselves. What does deceive mean? *(let them answer)* It means "to lie." What this means is like when I heard about the iron, but I lied to myself or deceived myself by thinking that I could do that later or just forget about the iron. I thought it would be okay, but you already told me what could happen if I didn't do something about the iron. I needed to do what the message said, not just hear it. That's what God is telling us in this verse. We need to do what God tells us to do and live our lives by God's guidelines, because when we do that, our lives are so much more meaningful. Let's remember this verse and do what God's word tells us, not just hear it.

Prayer

Dear God, thank you for all the times we can hear your word. Help us every day to do what your word tells us to do by loving you and each other. Amen.

Date: _____
Week 8

Philippians 4:13

I can do all things through him who strengthens me. — Philippians 4:13

Materials: a Bible, small weights or two cans to use as weights

I need a volunteer to be my personal trainer. I need you to encourage me and count the number of times I lift these weights. *(Encourage the child to say things like, keep it up, good job, harder, get going, and count, while lifting weights vigorously.)* Thank you for helping me. I've always wanted my own personal trainer. I know I'd work harder at this if I had someone to encourage me all the time. Why do you think I'm lifting these weights? *(let them answer)* I want to get stronger. What else could I do to become stronger? *(let them answer)* These things will help me build stronger muscles and have a strong body. What are some things I can do if I have a strong body? *(let them answer)*

Our verse for today talks about having a different kind of strength. It talks about being spiritually strong. I'll read it from the Bible. It's found in the New Testament, the book of Philippians, chapter 4, verse 13. *I can do all things through him who strengthens me.* *(have them repeat)*

God is like our very own personal trainer to help us become spiritually stronger. What are some of the ways God helps us become spiritually stronger? *(let them answer)* What are some things we can do if we are spiritually stronger? *(let them answer)* This verse says we can do all things through him who strengths us. This means that God is always with us to give us spiritual strength at all times in our life, when we have hard things to do, or difficult choices to make. We need to appreciate what we have.

Let's say this verse together. *I can do all things through him who strengthens me — Philippians 4:13.*

Prayer

Dear God, thank you for helping us become spiritually stronger and for always being with us. Help us to keep getting stronger spiritually by listening to your word, reading the Bible, and praying. Amen.

Date: _____
Week 9

1 Thessalonians 5:17

Pray without ceasing. — 1 Thessalonians 5:17

Materials: a Bible

Good morning! Oh, excuse me ... *(bow head in prayer).* Today I'd like to tell you that you're doing great on the B.I.B.L.E. verses. *(bow head in prayer)* This week's verse is from 1 Thessalonians 5:17 and I've been trying to do what it says *(bow head in prayer)*, but I can't get anything else done. *(bow head in prayer)* Maybe you could help me. *(bow head in prayer and say, "Excuse me, Jesus, but I've got to talk to these children.")* I'll read it from the Bible. It's in the New Testament, the book of 1 Thessalonians, chapter 5, verse 17. **Pray without ceasing.** *(have them repeat)* What I'm finding out is that praying constantly is very hard to do. I don't know how to pray without ceasing or all the time and still get the things done I need to do. Anyone have any suggestions? *(let them answer)*

To pray without ceasing doesn't mean I have to bow my head, close my eyes, and fold my hands all of the time, does it? To pray without ceasing can mean living my life with God always being a part of it, leading me and guiding me. There are times when I can bow my head and close my eyes and fold my hands. When are those times? *(let them answer)* There are definitely times when I should not pray with my head bowed, eyes closed, and hands folded. For instance, when I'm driving I pray a lot, but I need my head up, my eyes open, and my hands on the wheel. Prayer is communicating with God — living my life knowing God is right here all the time. We're praying right now as we listen to each other and offer answers and talk about this verse.

Let's say the verse again. ***Pray without ceasing — 1 Thessalonians 5:17.***

Let's practice this verse and become more aware of God being with us at all times. Now let's have a special prayer time together.

Prayer

Dear God, thank you for the times we can gather together to pray. We pray today for those who are sick and lonely. Help us to go through each day remembering you are with us. Amen.

Date: _____
Week 10

1 Thessalonians 5:25

Beloved, pray for us. — **1 Thessalonians 5:25**

Materials: a Bible, used get-well cards, a marker, and a board or large paper

Today I have a few of the get-well cards I received when I was sick some time ago. During that time, I asked people to pray for me. I had no idea how much those prayers would mean to me. I want to read what was written on a couple of the cards. "We're praying for you." "You're in our prayers." "I'm praying for you every day." Let me tell you, those cards really helped me. I felt so sick there were times I couldn't even pray for myself, but I knew there were other people out there praying for me. Knowing someone was praying for me helped me concentrate on getting better. It was such a comfort for me to know that someone cared enough about me to spend time praying for me.

I'll read our verse for today from the Bible. It's in the New Testament, in the book of 1 Thessalonians, chapter 5, verse 25. ***Beloved, pray for us.*** *(have them repeat)* There are times when people need some extra prayers. It's okay to ask others to pray for us. In this verse, the missionary Paul is asking the people at the church in Thessalonica to pray for him and those journeying with him. Let's say the verse again. ***Beloved, pray for us — 1 Thessalonians 5:25.***

When we know of someone needing extra prayers, we can ask others to pray for them, too. Let's make a list of those needing prayers today. *(write down names, ask congregation to add others)* Right now, let's do what this verse says.

Prayer

Dear God, we pray for *(name those on the list)*. We also take this moment to pray for those in our hearts. *(silent pause)* Thank you for the times others have prayed for us. Amen.

Date: _____
Week 11

Luke 12:34

For where your treasure is, there will your heart be also. — Luke 12:34

Materials: a Bible inside a chest or a suitcase with sign saying, "Treasure chest" on it

What I have today is a treasure chest. *(show them the treasure chest)* What do you think might be in a treasure chest? *(let them answer)* Sounds like those are some things you would like to have. But what if your treasure chest was to hold the thing that means the most to you? What would be in your treasure chest — what is most important in your life? *(let them answer)*

I put one of the most treasured items in my life inside this chest. Do you want to see what it is? *(let them answer, then show them)* It's the Bible! Our verse for today is about treasure. I'll read it from the Bible. It's in the New Testament, the book of Luke, chapter 12, verse 34. **For where your treasure is, there will your heart be also.** *(have them repeat)*

I put the Bible in my treasure chest because I want learning about God to be what is most important in my heart. What if I had chosen money to put in my treasure chest as most important? Even though I need money to buy food, clothes, and things, I don't want that to be the most important thing in my life. What if I put a brand new car in my treasure chest as most important? I need a car to get around, but again I don't want a car to be most important in my life. Our verse says that where our treasure is, what we think is most important in our life, that's where our hearts will be. I want God's love and teachings to be in my heart. We've been storing up more and more treasured verses of God's word in our hearts to help us learn how to live.

Let's say this once again. *For where your treasure is, there will your heart be also — Luke 12:34.*

Prayer

Dear God, help us to treasure your word and keep it in our hearts. Amen.

Date: _____
Week 12

Psalm 119:105

Your word is a lamp to my feet and a light to my path. — **Psalm 119:105**

Materials: a Bible, poster board made into a book cover with the following story printed on it

I have a special true story that I want to read to you today.

Light To My Path
by Anna L. Crane

Once upon a time there lived a little girl who had to go to church every week. There were times when she really didn't want to go, like when she was too tired or when she wanted to watch television or play outside, but every week she went with her family. The little girl learned Bible stories, memorized Bible verses, and the Lord's Prayer. She often wondered why she needed to learn all these things, especially when she didn't really understand what was being said.

One day, shortly after the girl graduated from high school, she was in a car accident. While trapped in her car, waiting for the emergency squad to arrive, she started to pray the Lord's Prayer, then she recited all of the Bible verses she had memorized as a child. With each verse she felt herself relax and become more and more calm. When the pain would feel worse, she would repeat over and over her favorite verse from Romans 8:28:

"We know that all things work together for good for those who love God, who are called according to his purpose." Remembering this verse reminded her that God was with her and that God could work good out of everything, even the accident. After she was released from the hospital, she thanked her parents for taking her to church as a little girl. It was the promises of God's love and his word that kept her calm during a very terrible time in her life.[1]

I'll read our verse for today from the Bible. It's in the Old Testament, the book of Psalms, chapter 119, verse 105. **Your word is a lamp to my feet and a light to my path.** *(have them repeat)* Knowing God's word and memorizing it does help us in times of need and when we have decisions to make — all the time, any time. God's word is like a lamp that gives us light to see what we need in life. How did God's word help the girl in the story? *(let them answer)* Knowing God's word can help you, too. Think about all of the verses we've learned this summer and how they can help us. *(name a few and ask, "How can that verse help us?")* God's word is a lamp to our feet and a light to our path of life, helping us and guiding us. This is our final week of the **Be Involved Bible Learners Everyone** program. I'd like you to think about all the verses you've learned and pick out your favorite one. Maybe some of you would like to share with us next week.

Let's say this verse. **Your word is a lamp to my feet and a light to my path — Psalm 119:105.**

Prayer
Dear God, thank you for lighting our path in life with your word. We are grateful that we are able to study your word and learn more about you. Amen.

---

1. Anna L. Crane is a pseudonym for a personal acquaintance.

Date: _____
Week 13

Our Favorites

Note: Ask the children to share their favorite verses and say why they are their favorites. Add a sentence or two about what the verse means. If no children respond, ask the adults to share their favorites. If no one shares, read a few verses of your choosing from the list asking who liked that one best and why.

Share the number of participants in the B.I.B.L.E. program, including how many memorized 6, 12, 18, 24, or more verses. Hand out awards or certificates at this time or mention that these will be at the back of church at the B.I.B.L.E. display for participants to pick up. Have those who memorized verses stand up. Recognize the oldest and youngest participants. Thank the volunteers who helped with the program.

Materials: a Bible, awards, and certificates

Even though this program is over, I hope that all of us will try to continue learning more of God's word and committing it to memory throughout the year and the rest of our lives. The message of God's love is always important, so please continue to be involved Bible learners, everyone.

Prayer
Dear God, thank you for the gift of your word in the Bible. Help us to continue reading and studying daily. May your word be a lamp to our feet and a light to our path. Amen.

B.I.B.L.E. Chairperson Checklist

- Set dates for the B.I.B.L.E. program.

- Choose a place for a display.

- Supply list: six poster boards, paints or markers, index cards and file box, sturdy shoe box, paper for copies, pens, tape or poster putty.

- Decide if a celebration event will mark the end of the B.I.B.L.E. program. This event may be refreshments after church on the last Sunday, a carry-in dinner, thank-you ceremony, reception for participants.

- Send letter to Christian educators.

- Recruit volunteers to help with the B.I.B.L.E. program. Use volunteer sign-up sheet for Sunday helpers.

- Give children's sermon material to the person or people who are going to present them during worship services. Some suggestions might be clergy, youth workers, Christian educators, lay volunteers, or committee members.

- Make posters.

- Copy name tags and cut out.

- Copy memory papers and cut out.

- Decorate memory box.

- Begin publishing bulletin/newsletter material three weeks before the B.I.B.L.E. program starts.

❏ Make a master list on an index card for each participant to be placed in a file box alphabetically. This is an easy way to keep track of the verses each participant has memorized and to make sure the name tags on the display are in the correct spot.

❏ Set up the display the week before the B.I.B.L.E. program begins.

❏ Once the B.I.B.L.E. program has begun, record verses placed in the memory box on the master list and on name tags, moving the name tag under the appropriate poster each week.

❏ Before the final week of the B.I.B.L.E. program, copy certificates, filling them out, and purchase or make prizes if using these items.

❏ Finalize celebration event if planning one.

Sample Letter
To Christian Educators

Greetings of Peace,

Our congregation will be participating in the B.I.B.L.E. program during the next several weeks, memorizing one verse from the Bible per week. We want to help our children be successful and enjoy this program, so we need your help. The following explains how your department can make the most of the value of memorizing God's word.

1. Each Sunday, the verse for the week will be written out on a poster and repeated in unison during the opening. We will also look it up in the Bible.
2. Make copies of the verse to send home with the children to work on during the week. In older classes, have the students write out the verse to take home.
3. On the following Sunday, the children can recite their verse to any teacher who will fill out the memory paper and put it in the memory box by the display. This will help keep the volunteers by the display from being overwhelmed by too many reciting at once.
4. Each Sunday, during worship, the children's sermon will center on the week's verse bringing the whole program together.
5. We will have certificates available to hand out to students who have memorized 6, 12, 18, 24, or more verses.

Thank you for helping with this program. Knowing God's word is a wonderful thing for all of us to **Be Involved Bible Learners Everyone.**

In Christ's Love,

B.I.B.L.E. Chairperson

Sample Bulletin/Newsletter Announcements

Bulletin or newsletter notices to be used to announce and explain the B.I.B.L.E. program.

Date _____
4 weeks before
   Be on the lookout for the B.I.B.L.E. coming the week of _____. Anyone interested in learning more about the B.I.B.L.E. or willing to help with this special project call the church office.

Date _____
3 weeks before
   B.I.B.L.E. will be here on _____! This new program will be open for everyone's enjoyment for twelve weeks. The letters stand for **Be Involved Bible Learners Everyone**. This is a great opportunity for all of us, young and old, to learn more about the Bible. For more details see next Sunday's bulletin.

Date _____
2 weeks before
   B.I.B.L.E. (**Be Involved Bible Learners Everyone**) is almost here! The art of memorization is all but gone in this age of calculators and computers. There are times when having something committed to memory helps us in life. We are challenged to memorize one Bible verse per week. Having God's word in our heart and on our mind can help us in decision-making, times of joy, and hardships. Watch for the B.I.B.L.E. display in church next week.

Date _____
Introduction week
   B.I.B.L.E. (**Be Involved Bible Learners Everyone**) On your mark, get set, go to your Bible and start getting to know God's word

through memorization. Everyone is welcome to join the challenge. Each week, before and after church, someone will be at the B.I.B.L.E. display to listen to the Bible verse you have memorized. Your name will be put up under the first poster and moved ahead for every verse you complete. You can go through the twelve-week course as many times as you like, don't stop at just twelve verses! There are suggested verses at the display if you need a little help or choose your own favorites. There are also suggested verses for our little ones. Come on kids, challenge your parents and make this a family project. Seniors and singles pair up with a friend or a teen and take the challenge. (Everyone memorizing six verses will receive something special for their achievement.) The verse for this week is: *Let all that you do be done in love — 1 Corinthians 16:14.*

Date _____
Week 1

B.I.B.L.E. Helpful hint to memorization: First, read the verse silently, next out loud, and then with your eyes closed. Repeat this process daily. The verse for this week is: *Rejoice in the Lord always; again I will say, Rejoice — Philippians 4:4.*

Date _____
Week 2

B.I.B.L.E. It's great to see new names popping up each week. Keep the challenge going. The verse for this week is: *For God so loved the world that he gave his only Son, so that everyone who believes in him may not perish but may have eternal life — John 3:16.*

Date _____
Week 3

B.I.B.L.E. Did you remember to memorize a Bible verse this week? Go to the display and recite your verse to the adult and move your name tag along memory lane. The verse for this week is: *We love, because he first loved us — 1 John 4:19.*

Date _____
Week 4

B.I.B.L.E. There are so many great verses in God's word. Find one on your own or memorize this week's choice. The verse for this week is: *Thanks be to God for his indescribable gift! — 2 Corinthians 9:15.*

Date _____
Week 5

B.I.B.L.E. Helpful hint to memorization: After the verse is committed to memory, repeat it before each meal and at bedtime. The verse for this week is: *Jesus Christ is the same yesterday and today and forever — Hebrews 13:8.*

Date _____
Week 6

B.I.B.L.E. It's not too late to join the challenge; you can sign up at anytime. The verse for this week is: *Jesus wept — John 11:35* **(RSV).**

Date _____
Week 7

B.I.B.L.E. Invite someone new to take the B.I.B.L.E. challenge. The verse for this week is: *But be doers of the word, and not merely hearers who deceive themselves — James 1:22.*

Date _____
Week 8

B.I.B.L.E. When you recite your verse thank the volunteer that listens to you. The verse for this week is: *I can do all things through him who strengthens me — Philippians 4:13.*

Date _____
Week 9

B.I.B.L.E. Helpful hint to memorization: See how many times you can recite the verse during supper each night. The verse for this week is: *Pray without ceasing — 1 Thessalonians 5:17.*

Date _____
Week 10

B.I.B.L.E. Only a few weeks left; keep learning those verses. The verse for this week is: *Beloved, pray for us — **1 Thessalonians 5:25.***

Date _____
Week 11

B.I.B.L.E. Greet someone with a Bible verse today. The verse for this week is: ***For where your treasure is, there will your heart be also — Luke 12:34.***

Date _____
Week 12

B.I.B.L.E. Next week we will honor all those participating in this summer program. During the week think about your favorite verse. The verse for this week is: ***Your word is a lamp to my feet and a light to my path — Psalm 119:105.***

Date _____
Week 13

B.I.B.L.E. A big thank you goes to the volunteers who organized, listened, and helped in any way with this special program. Congratulations to all the participants of the B.I.B.L.E. Even though this is the last week, continue to learn more about God's word and keep it in your heart always. *(A note of thanks to the volunteers and a list of names of participants may be added to the bulletin notice.)*

B.I.B.L.E. Display Ideas

1. Set up the display in the back of the sanctuary, in the fellowship hall, in a hallway, or anyplace that will be visible to the congregation and easily accessible to those wanting to recite verses.

2. It is helpful to have a table and chairs for the volunteers to sit on when they are listening to and recording memorized verses.

3. Keep a master list of all participants with names and the verses memorized on index cards in a file box, filed alphabetically.

4. Use Bible name cards to record verses and move along the twelve-poster display.

5. Cover a shoebox and cut an opening in the top to place memory papers filled out by a Sunday school teacher during class, by parents, and so on to be recorded at a convenient time.

6. Have name tags, memory papers, pens, and tape on the table.

7. Cut six large poster boards in half and use one of the ideas below to set up the display where participant's name tags will be posted.

    - Write the verse of the week on each poster. Cut the poster in the shape of an open Bible.

    - Invite an artist in the congregation or children of the church to draw and color pictures depicting the life of Jesus: birth, in the temple as a boy, baptism, miracle of water into wine, sermon on the mount, walking on water, raising of Lazarus, Palm Sunday, Lord's Supper, praying in Gethsemane, crucifixion, and Easter.

- Invite an artist in the congregation or children of the church to draw and color pictures depicting Old and New Testament stories: Adam and Eve, Noah, Tower of Babel, Moses, David and Goliath, Jonah and the whale, Jesus' birth, miracle of water into wine, the crucifixion, Easter, Pentecost, and a map of Christianity.

- Use symbols of the church: cross, shell of baptism, alpha and omega, three intertwined circles of the trinity, butterfly for new life, dove of peace, bread and wine for communion, fish, heart, angel, world, and praying hands.

- Use the symbols of the twelve disciples. These can be found at various sites online.

B.I.B.L.E. Procedure Explanation Poster

B.I.B.L.E.

1. Memorize a Bible verse.

2. Recite the Bible verse from memory to a parent, Christian Educator, or volunteer at this display.

3. Write your name and Bible verse on the memory paper, and have the adult listening sign and date it.

4. Place the memory paper in the memory box.

5. Your name will be placed under the appropriate B.I.B.L.E. poster each week.

```
Name   Paul Smith

Bible Verse   John 3:16

Signed by   Cindy Lane

Date   June 1
```

B.I.B.L.E. Volunteer Sign-Up Sheet

Two volunteers are needed each Sunday to listen to and record participants' Bible verses.

Week 1: Date _____

_____   _____

Week 2: Date _____

_____   _____

Week 3: Date _____

_____   _____

Week 4: Date _____

_____   _____

Week 5: Date _____

_____   _____

Week 6: Date _____

_____   _____

Week 7: Date _____

_____ _____

Week 8: Date _____

_____ _____

Week 9: Date _____

_____ _____

Week 10: Date _____

_____ _____

Week 11: Date _____

_____ _____

Week 12: Date _____

_____ _____

Bible Verses For Little Ones Master Sheet

Let all that you do be done in love.
— 1 Corinthians 16:14

Rejoice in the Lord always; again I will say, Rejoice. — Philippians 4:4

For God so loved the world that he gave his only Son, so that everyone who believes in him may not perish but may have eternal life.
— John 3:16

We love, because he first loved us.
— 1 John 4:19

Thanks be to God for his indescribable gift!
— 2 Corinthians 9:15

Jesus Christ is the same yesterday and today and forever. — Hebrews 13:8

Jesus wept. — John 11:35 (RSV)

But be doers of the word, and not merely hearers who deceive themselves. — James 1:22

I can do all things through him who strengthens me. — Philippians 4:13

Pray without ceasing. — 1 Thessalonians 5:17

Beloved, pray for us. — 1 Thessalonians 5:25

For where your treasure is, there will your heart be also.   — Luke 12:34

Your word is a lamp to my feet and a light to my path.   — Psalm 119:105

Let mutual love continue.   — Hebrews 13:1

I am the bread of life.   — John 6:48

Judge not, that you be not judged.
   — Matthew 7:1 (RSV)

He must increase, but I must decrease.
   — John 3:30

For many are called, but few are chosen.
   — Matthew 22:14

For the Son of Man came to seek out and to save the lost.   — Luke 19:10

More Suggested Verses For B.I.B.L.E. Master Sheet

Genesis:	1:1, 3, 6, 9, 14, 20, 24, 26, 31; 2:2; 9:12, 13
Exodus:	20:2, 3, 4, 7, 8, 12, 13, 14, 15, 16, 17
Ruth:	1:16
Psalms:	23:1, 2, 3, 4, 5, 6; 111:1; 150:1, 2, 3, 4, 5, 6
Proverbs:	2:20; 3:13, 14; 10:12; 15:1
Ecclesiastes:	3:1, 2, 3, 4, 5, 6, 7, 8
Daniel:	6:22
Matthew:	5:3, 4, 5, 7, 8, 9, 10, 11, 16; 7:3, 7, 14; 10:42; 11:28, 29, 30; 18:4, 20; 19:14; 20:26, 27, 28
Mark:	1:8, 17; 16:16
Luke:	2:10; 6:27; 11:28
John:	3:16, 17; 10:11; 13:35; 14:1, 27; 15:13
Romans:	1:16; 6:23; 7:15; 8:28; 12:12, 21
1 Corinthians:	3:7; 10:13; 13:4, 13
Galatians:	5:25
Ephesians:	2:8, 9

Philippians:	4:8, 13
Hebrews:	11:1
James:	1:22; 3:17
1 Peter:	4:9; 5:7

Master List And Name Tag Example Sheet

Smith, Matthew		
1. Phil. 4:4	9.	17.
2. Eph. 6:1	10.	18.
3. Jn. 11:35	11.	19.
4.	12.	20.
5.	13.	21.
6.	14.	22.
7.	15.	23.
8.	16.	24.

(Index card to be alphabetized in file box.)

Matthew's name tag would be under poster number three.

Matthew Smith	
1. Phil. 4:4	7.
2. Eph. 6:1	8.
3. Jn. 11:35	9.
4.	10.
5.	11.
6.	12.

Jones, Philip		
1. Phil. 4:4	9. Ex. 20:1	17. Jn. 3:16
2. Eph. 6:1	10. Eph. 2:8	18.
3. Jn. 11:35	11. Jn. 14:1	19.
4. Mt. 5:3	12. Lk. 2:10	20.
5. Mk. 1:8	13. Mt. 7:7	21.
6. Jn. 3:17	14. Ps. 100:1	22.
7. James 1:22	15. Mt. 20:6	23.
8. Gen. 1:1	16. Eph. 6:1	24.

(Index card to be alphabetized in file box.)

Philip's name tags would be under poster number five.

Philip Jones	
1. Phil. 4:4	7. James 1:22
2. Eph. 6:1	8. Gen. 1:1
3. Jn. 11:35	9. Ex. 20:1
4. Mt. 5:3	10. Eph. 2:8
5. Mk. 1:8	11. Jn. 14:1
6. Jn. 3:17	12. Lk. 2:10

Philip Jones	
13. Mt. 7:7	19.
14. Ps. 100:1	20.
15. Mt. 20:6	21.
16. Eph. 6:1	22.
17. Jn. 3:16	23.
18.	24.

(After completing 12 verses, place double name tag under poster one and begin the route again.)

Attach two name tags together.

Memory Paper Example Sheet

Name Philip Jones

Bible Verse   Matthew 20:6

Signed by *Cindy Lane*

Date   August 3

The memory paper would be placed in the memory file box and when recorded, Philip's name would move to the next poster.

Memory Paper Master Sheet

Name _____

Bible Verse _____

Signed by _____

Date _____

Name _____

Bible Verse _____

Signed by _____

Date _____

Name _____

Bible Verse _____

Signed by _____

Date _____

Name	_____
Bible Verse	_____
Signed by	_____
Date	_____

Name	_____
Bible Verse	_____
Signed by	_____
Date	_____

Name	_____
Bible Verse	_____
Signed by	_____
Date	_____

Name Tag Master Sheet

Name	
1.	7.
2.	8.
3.	9.
4.	10.
5.	11.
6.	12.

Name	
13.	19.
14.	20.
15.	21.
16.	22.
16.	23.
18.	24.

Name	
1.	7
2.	8.
3.	9.
4.	10.
5.	11.
6.	12.

Name	
13.	19.
14.	20.
15.	21.
16.	22.
17.	23.
18.	24.

Name	
1.	7.
2.	8.
3.	9.
4.	10.
5.	11.
6.	12.

Name	
13.	19.
14.	20.
15.	21.
16.	22.
16.	23.
18.	24.

Name	
1.	7
2.	8.
3.	9.
4.	10.
5.	11.
6.	12.

Name	
13.	19.
14.	20.
15.	21.
16.	22.
17.	23.
18.	24.

Sample Certificate

Other special incentives may be awarded, but keep the main focus on memorizing and understanding God's word.

Incentive prize ideas: balloons, bookmarks, posters, erasers, pencils, and similar gifts.

www.ingramcontent.com/pod-product-compliance
Lightning Source LLC
Chambersburg PA
CBHW071757040426
42446CB00012B/2591